KITCHEN JOURNAL

KITCHEN JOURNAL

Custard: A detestable substance produced by a malevolent conspiracy of the hen, the cow, and the cook.

Ambrose Bierce (1842–1914)

RECIPES FROM FRIENDS AND FAMILY

If God had intended us to follow recipes,
He wouldn't have given us grandmothers.

Linda Henley

RECIPES FROM FRIENDS AND FAMILY

The most remarkable thing about my mother is that for thirty years she served the family nothing but leftovers. The original meal has never been found.

Calvin Trillin

Use the following pages to write recipes and tips you have been given. Recipes which have been passed down through the family or from friend to friend are often the most satisfying to use. They are a link with our past and can be passed on to future generations and enjoyed as the years go by.

INGREDIENTS

METHOD

INGREDIENTS

METHOD

recipes from friends and family

INGREDIENTS

METHOD

INGREDIENTS

METHOD

INGREDIENTS

METHOD

INGREDIENTS

METHOD

INGREDIENTS

METHOD

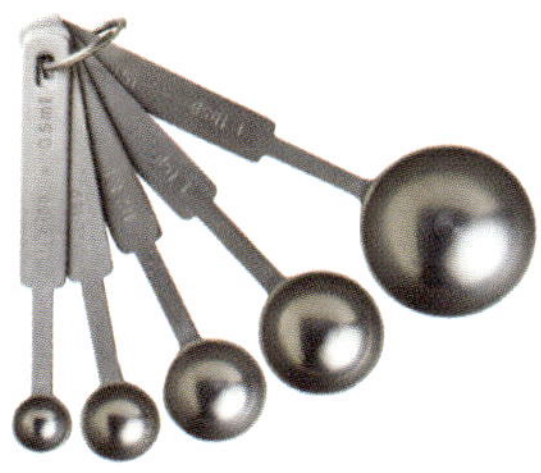

INGREDIENTS

METHOD

EVERYDAY ESSENTIALS

There is no love sincerer than the love of food.

George Bernard Shaw (1856–1950),
The Revolutionist's Handbook, *Man and Superman*

EVERYDAY ESSENTIALS

Bread deals with living things, with giving life, with growth, with the seed, the grain that nurtures. It is not coincidence that we say bread is the staff of life.

Lionel Poilane (1945–2002)

The following pages include the basic conversion charts for weighing, measuring and temperatures. These are good to refer to when translating from old recipe books, recipes you have been given and recipes from parts of the world where the method of measuring is different.

There are also pages for writing basic recipes which you can refer to on a day-to-day basis – use these for the recipes you tend to use frequently in your cooking or as a quick reference to jog your memory.

OVEN TEMPERATURES

FAHRENHEIT	CENTIGRADE	GAS MARK	DESCRIPTION
225 F	105 C	1/4	Very Cool
250 F	120 C	1/2	
275 F	130 C	1	Cool
300 F	150 C	2	
325 F	165 C	3	Very Moderate
350 F	180 C	4	Moderate
375 F	190 C	5	
400 F	200 C	6	Moderately Hot
425 F	220 C	7	Hot
450 F	230 C	8	
475 F	245 C	9	Very Hot

CONVERSION TABLES

WEIGHING AND MEASURING

CUPS	TSP	TBSP	LB/OZ	KG/G	PINTS/FL OZ	L/ML
	⅕					1 ml
	1	⅓				5 ml
1/16	3	1			½ fl oz	15 ml
⅛	6	2			1 fl oz	30 ml
¼	12	4			2 fl oz	60 ml
½		8			4 fl oz	120 ml
¾		12			6 fl oz	180 ml
1		16			½ pint/8 fl oz	240 ml
2		32			1 pint	470 ml
4					2 pints	950 ml
4.2					2.1 pints	1 litre
			1 oz	28 g		
			2 oz	55 g		
			3 oz	85 g		
			3.5 oz	100 g		
			¼ lb/4 oz	125 g		
			1 lb/16 oz	454 g		
			2 lb/32 oz	907 g		
			2.2 lb/35 oz	1 kg		

Note: There is a big difference between fluid ounces which is a volume measurement and dry ounces which is a weight measurement, so check your recipes carefully before weighing and measuring ingredients.

INGREDIENTS

METHOD

INGREDIENTS

METHOD

INGREDIENTS

METHOD

INGREDIENTS

METHOD

INGREDIENTS

METHOD

INGREDIENTS

METHOD

INGREDIENTS

METHOD

INGREDIENTS

METHOD

TASTY EXPERIMENTS

When baking, follow directions. When cooking, go by your own taste.

Laiko Bahrs

SANTA
RECIOTO
SANTA

TASTY EXPERIMENTS

But when the time comes that a man has had his dinner,
then the true man comes to the surface.

Mark Twain (1835–1910)

Use the following pages to note down the cooking experiments that have been successful. It is frustrating when you make a delicious dish by chance and can't remember how you did it!

INGREDIENTS

METHOD

INGREDIENTS

METHOD

tasty experiments

INGREDIENTS

METHOD

INGREDIENTS

METHOD

INGREDIENTS

METHOD

INGREDIENTS

METHOD

INGREDIENTS

METHOD

INGREDIENTS

METHOD

INGREDIENTS

METHOD

INGREDIENTS

METHOD

SNACKS AND STARTERS

This is every cook's opinion –
no savory dish without an onion,
but lest your kissing should be spoiled
your onions must be fully boiled.

Jonathan Swift (1667–1745)

SNACKS AND STARTERS

Many's the long night I've dreamed of cheese – toasted, mostly.

Robert Louis Stevenson (1850–1894)

INGREDIENTS

METHOD

INGREDIENTS

METHOD

INGREDIENTS

METHOD

INGREDIENTS

METHOD

INGREDIENTS

METHOD

INGREDIENTS

METHOD

INGREDIENTS

METHOD

INGREDIENTS

METHOD

INGREDIENTS

METHOD

INGREDIENTS

METHOD

MAIN COURSES

Tell me what you eat, I'll tell you who you are.

Anthelme Brillat-Savarin (1755–1826)

MAIN COURSES

Some hae meat and canna eat,
And some would eat that want it;
But we hae meat, and we can eat,
Sae let the Lord be thankit.

Robert Burns (1759–1796), *Grace before Meat*

INGREDIENTS

METHOD

INGREDIENTS

METHOD

INGREDIENTS

METHOD

INGREDIENTS

METHOD

INGREDIENTS

METHOD

INGREDIENTS

METHOD

INGREDIENTS

METHOD

INGREDIENTS

METHOD

INGREDIENTS

METHOD

DESSERTS AND SWEET THINGS

After dinner sit a while, and after supper walk a mile.

English saying

DESSERTS AND SWEET THINGS

Cookies are made of butter and love.

Norwegian Proverb

INGREDIENTS

METHOD

INGREDIENTS

METHOD

INGREDIENTS

METHOD

INGREDIENTS

METHOD

INGREDIENTS

METHOD

INGREDIENTS

METHOD

INGREDIENTS

METHOD

INGREDIENTS

METHOD

INGREDIENTS

METHOD

INGREDIENTS

METHOD

SEASONAL PRODUCE

There are only ten minutes in the life of a pear when it is perfect to eat.

Ralph Waldo Emerson (1803–1882)

garden fresh

SEASONAL PRODUCE

Always eat grapes downward – that is eat the best grapes first; in this way there will be none better left on the bunch, and each grape will seem good down to the last. If you eat the other way, you will not have a good grape in the lot.

Samuel Butler (1612–1680)

Use the following pages to make lists of fresh ingredients and when it comes into season. Often buying seasonal produce makes shopping for food cheaper because it is readily available. It also helps to ensure you are buying the freshest possible ingredients; seasonal produce is often locally sourced so the transportation costs are lower and the possibility of the produce being in cold storage for long periods is reduced.

seasonal produce

JANUARY

FEBRUARY

seasonal produce

MARCH

PEAS

seasonal produce

APRIL

MAY

seasonal produce

JUNE

seasonal produce

JULY

AUGUST

seasonal produce

SEPTEMBER

seasonal produce

OCTOBER

seasonal produce

NOVEMBER

DECEMBER

LIKES AND DISLIKES

An empty belly is the best cook.

Estonian proverb

LIKES AND DISLIKES

He was a very valiant man who first adventured on eating oysters.

James I

Use the following pages to make a note of the likes and dislikes of the people you know. This will make life much easier when preparing a meal for them. Many people have allergies or intolerances to certain foods and having these to hand when preparing food can avoid an awkward situation when you sit down to eat and prevent the sad waste of a good meal.

likes and dislikes

NAME

LIKES

DISLIKES

ALLERGIES

NAME

LIKES

DISLIKES

ALLERGIES

NAME

LIKES

DISLIKES

ALLERGIES

likes and dislikes

NAME

LIKES

DISLIKES

ALLERGIES

NAME

LIKES

DISLIKES

ALLERGIES

NAME

LIKES

DISLIKES

ALLERGIES

likes and dislikes

NAME

LIKES

DISLIKES

ALLERGIES

NAME

LIKES

DISLIKES

ALLERGIES

NAME

LIKES

DISLIKES

ALLERGIES

likes and dislikes

NAME

LIKES

DISLIKES

ALLERGIES

NAME

LIKES

DISLIKES

ALLERGIES

NAME

LIKES

DISLIKES

ALLERGIES

likes and dislikes

NAME

LIKES

DISLIKES

ALLERGIES

NAME

LIKES

DISLIKES

ALLERGIES

NAME

LIKES

DISLIKES

ALLERGIES

likes and dislikes

NAME

LIKES

DISLIKES

ALLERGIES

NAME

LIKES

DISLIKES

ALLERGIES

NAME

LIKES

DISLIKES

ALLERGIES

PULTENEY
PRESS

Published in 2008 by Pulteney Press,
1 Riverside Court, St John's Road, Bath BA2 6PD

Designed and produced for Pulteney Press
by Open Door Limited, Rutland UK

ISBN: 978 1906734183